Angels

A B O O K O F P O S T C A R D S

POMEGRANATE ARTBOOKS / SAN FRANCISCO

Pomegranate Artbooks
Box 6099
Rohnert Park, CA 94927

ISBN 1-56640-960-8
Pomegranate Catalog No. A707

Pomegranate publishes books of postcards on a wide variety of subjects.
Please write to the publisher for more information.
© 1994 Pomegranate Artbooks

Designed by Mark Koenig
Printed in Korea

06 05 04 03 02 01 00 99   16 15 14 13 12 11 10 9

Outside the open window
The morning air is all awash with angels.
— Richard Purdy Wilbur,
Love Calls Us to the Things of This World, 1956

The term *angel* derives from a Greek translation of the Hebrew word *mal'akh,* which originally meant "the shadow side of God" but later came to mean "messenger." Thus, in Western tradition at least, the primary significance of angels lies not in who or what they are but in what they do — communicate God's word to humankind.

Whether serving as heavenly messengers, guardians or intermediaries, angels represent a particularly lustrous common thread in the tapestry of human belief. They appear in ancient Greek myths, in Hinduism and Buddhism, in the writings of Sufi mystics and in Native American legends, and in the traditional beliefs of Islam, Judaism and Christianity. The Bible makes numerous references to them: in the Old Testament, Jacob wrestles with an angel and an angel prevents Abraham from sacrificing his son; in the New Testament, the archangel Gabriel gives notice to Mary that she will be the mother of Christ. Hebrews 13:1–2 reminds us, "Be not forgetful to entertain strangers: for thereby some have entertained angels unawares." To this day, belief in angels remains strong: while some scoff at the idea, others claim to have seen and spoken with angels. Modern mystics receive angels through channeling and as extraterrestrial visitors.

Throughout history, artists have tapped this reservoir of collective belief and created images of stunning beauty, images that inspire us, presenting angels as symbols of beauty, compassion and grace. The exquisite paintings in this collection of postcards are interpretations of celestial beings by twenty-five renowned artists, from Pre-Raphaelites such as Edward Burne-Jones and Evelyn de Morgan to contemporary painters such as Wolfgang Grässe and Susan Seddon Boulet. Whatever their individual styles, the painters' reverence for their subject matter is evident in the angels' delicate features and in the hushed and peaceful aura surrounding them. We may not know exactly how an angel would look, but these images give us a powerful vision of possibility.

Angels

Abbott Handerson Thayer (American, 1849–1921)
Angel, 1889
Oil on canvas, 36¼ x 28⅛ in.

Pomegranate. Box 6099, Rohnert Park, CA 94927

Angels

Annie Swynnerton (English, 1844–1933)
Cupid and Psyche (detail)

Pomegranate, Box 6099, Rohnert Park, CA 94927

Angels

Hugo Simberg (Finnish, 1873–1917)
Wounded Angel, 1903
Oil on canvas, 50 x 60⅝ in.

Pomegranate, Box 6099, Rohnert Park, CA 94927

Angels

Gillian Lawson (British)
Angels (detail), 1990
Watercolor, 12 x 10 in.

Pomegranate, Box 6099, Rohnert Park, CA 94927

Angels

Sir Edward Burne-Jones (English, 1833–1898)
Angel

Pomegranate, Box 6099, Rohnert Park, CA 94927

Angels

John William Waterhouse (English, 1849–1917)
The Annunciation

Pomegranate, Box 6099, Rohnert Park, CA 94927

Angels
William Edward Frank Britten (1848–1916)
Two Angels

Pomegranate, Box 6099, Rohnert Park, CA 94927

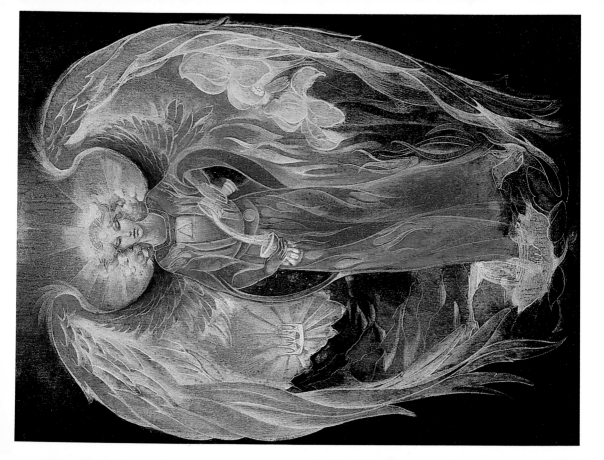

Angels

Susan Seddon Boulet (Brazilian, b. 1941)
Angel
Oil pastel, ink and pencil

Pomegranate, Box 6099, Rohnert Park, CA 94927

Angels

John Duncan (Scottish, 1866–1945)
St. Bride, 1913
Tempera on canvas, 48½ x 57½ in.

Pomegranate, Box 6099, Rohnert Park, CA 94927

Angels

Ann Macbeth (Scottish)
The Nativity, c. 1940
Embroidered silk and wool, blue and clear glass beads on
linen, 46½ x 55¾ in.

Pomegranate, Box 6099, Rohnert Park, CA 94927

Angels

Wolfgang Grässe (Australian, b. Germany 1930)
Altar of Angels III (detail), 1987
Oil on panel

Pomegranate, Box 6099, Rohnert Park, CA 94927

Angels

Niki Broyles (American, b. 1947)
Angel and the Snow Unicorn (detail), 1980
Acrylic on canvas

Pomegranate, Box 6099, Rohnert Park, CA 94927

Angels

Sir Edward Burne-Jones (English, 1833–1898)
The Days of Creation (The First Day) (detail)
Watercolor, shell gold (metallic paint) and gouache on
linen, mounted on paper, 40⅛ x 14 in.

Pomegranate, Box 6099, Rohnert Park, CA 94927

Angels

Matthew Ridley Corbett (1850–1902)
Psyche Loses Sight of Love (detail)

Pomegranate, Box 6099, Rohnert Park, CA 94927

Angels

Frank Cadogan Cowper (English, 1877–1958)
Francis of Assisi and the Heavenly Melody
Oil on canvas

Pomegranate, Box 6099, Rohnert Park, CA 94927

Angels

Sir Edward Burne-Jones (English, 1833–1898)
The Annunciation: Angel Gabriel

Pomegranate, Box 6099, Rohnert Park, CA 94927

Angels

Cliff McReynolds (American, b. 1933)
Day (detail), 1975
Oil on canvas, 12 x 12 in.

Pomegranate, Box 6099, Rohnert Park, CA 94927

Angels

Franz Karl Delavilla (German, 1884–1967)
Frohe Weihnachten (Merry Christmas) (detail)
Number 19 in a series of postcards published by the
Wiener Werkstätte (Vienna Workshop), 1907–1914

Pomegranate, Box 6099, Rohnert Park, CA 94927

Angels

Frederick Judd Waugh (American, 1861–1914)
The Knight of the Holy Grail, 1912
Oil on canvas, 94¾ x 125¾ in.

Pomegranate, Box 6099, Rohnert Park, CA 94927

Angels

Sidney Harold Meteyard (1868–1947)
Eros, Love in Idleness (detail)

Pomegranate, Box 6099, Rohnert Park, CA 94927

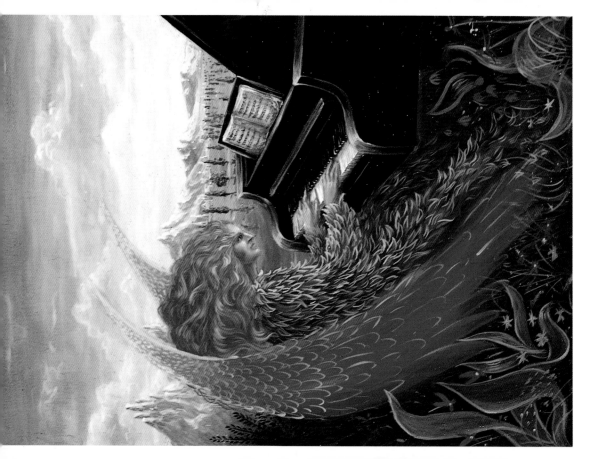

Angels
Václav Váca (Canadian, b. Czechoslovakia 1948)
Grand Piano (detail), 1979
Oil on canvas, 12 x 18 in.

Pomegranate, Box 6099, Rohnert Park, CA 94927

Angels

John Melhuish Strudwick (1849–1937)
The Ramparts of God's House (detail)

Pomegranate, Box 6099, Rohnert Park, CA 94927

Angels

Armand Point (1860–1932)
The Siren (detail), 1897
Oil on canvas

Pomegranate, Box 6099, Rohnert Park, CA 94927

Angels

Abbott Handerson Thayer (American, 1849–1921)
Winged Figure Seated upon a Rock
Oil on canvas, 213.5 x 153.0 cm

Pomegranate. Box 6099, Rohnert Park, CA 94927

Angels

Arthur Hacker (English, 1858–1919)
The Cloister or the World

Pomegranate, Box 6099, Rohnert Park, CA 94927

Angels

Wolfgang Grässe (Australian, b. Germany 1930)
Adoration of the Magi, 1991
Acrylic on masonite, 16 x 13 in.

Pomegranate, Box 6099, Rohnert Park, CA 94927

Angels

Melozzo da Forli (Italian, 1438–1494)
Angel Musician

Pomegranate, Box 6099, Rohnert Park, CA 94927

POMEGRANATE BOOKS OF POSTCARDS
ON MUSIC AND POPULAR CULTURE

Pomegranate publishes books of postcards on a wide range of subjects.
Please write to the publisher foar more information.

Whether serving as heavenly messengers, guardians or intermediaries, angels represent a particularly lustrous common thread in the tapestry of human belief. Throughout history, artists have tapped this reservoir of collective belief and created images of stunning beauty, presenting angels as symbols of transcendant compassion and grace. Whatever their individual styles, the painters' reverence for their subject matter is evident in the angels' delicate features and in the hushed and peaceful aura surrounding them. We may not know exactly how an angel would look, but these images give us a powerful vision of possibility.

ISBN 1-56640-960-8

$9.95

9 781566 409605

7 17194 00707 3

Contains thirty oversized postcards
Pomegranate Artbooks A707